The Bizarre Body

By Katharine Kenah

School Specialty Publishing

Columbus, Ohio

Copyright © 2005 School Specialty Publishing, a member of the School
Specialty Family.

Printed in the United States of America. All rights reserved. Except as permitted
under the United States Copyright Act, no part of this publication may be
reproduced or distributed in any form or by any means, or stored in a database or
retrieval system, without prior written permission from the publisher, unless
otherwise indicated.

Library of Congress Cataloging-in-Publication Data is on file with the publisher.

Send all inquiries to:
School Specialty Publishing
8720 Orion Place
Columbus, OH 43240-2111

ISBN 0-7696-3180-0

3 4 5 6 7 8 PHX 09 08 07 06 05

The human body
is a wonderful machine.
It can see and hear.
It can taste and touch.
It can run and jump.
It can think and dream.

The human body is beautiful,
surprising, and sometimes bizarre.

Tongue

Your tongue can change shape.
It moves around in your mouth.
This helps you eat and talk.
Tiny bumps on your tongue
are called *taste buds*.
They tell your brain when food
is sweet, sour, bitter, or salty.

Weird Facts

- The tongue is one of the strongest muscles in the human body.

- The pattern of taste buds on your tongue is one of a kind. No one else has the same tongue print!

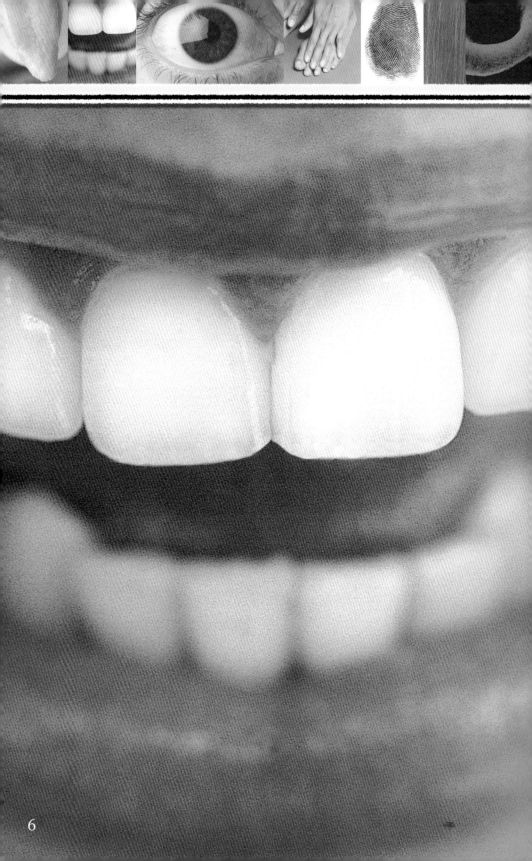

Teeth

You are born with two sets of teeth.
They are under your gums.
Twenty baby teeth grow in first.
They fall out one by one.
Later, thirty-two adult teeth grow in.
Different teeth have different jobs.
They work together to chew up food.

Weird Facts

- The hardest thing in the human body is tooth enamel.
- George Washington's false teeth were made of ivory and gold, not wood.

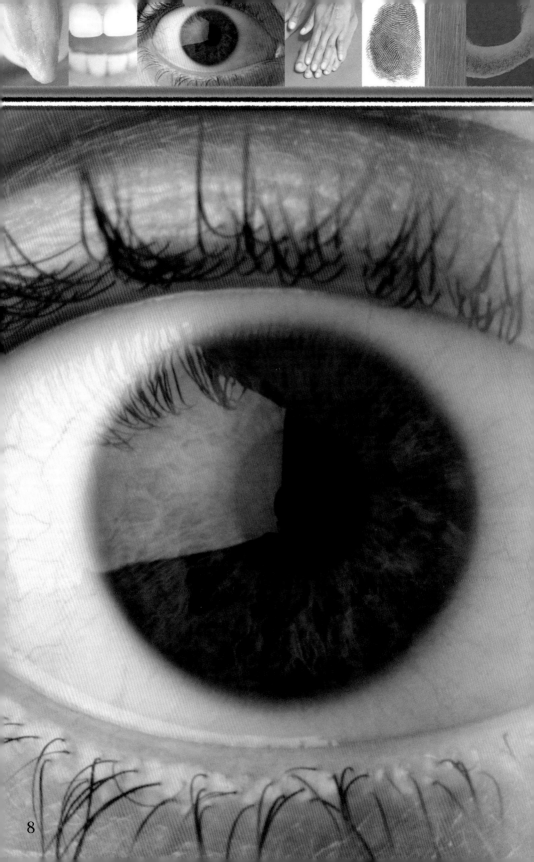

Eyes

Your eyes show you the world.
You use your eyes
for almost everything you do.
Eyeballs are only about one-inch wide.
They can see faraway things,
like stars, or things nearby, like flowers.
Your eyes cannot see anything
in total darkness.

Weird Facts

- If you lose sight in one eye, you lose only one-fifth of your vision. Your other eye will make up for some of the lost sight.

- Your eyes receive images upside down. Your brain turns them right-side-up before you "see" them.

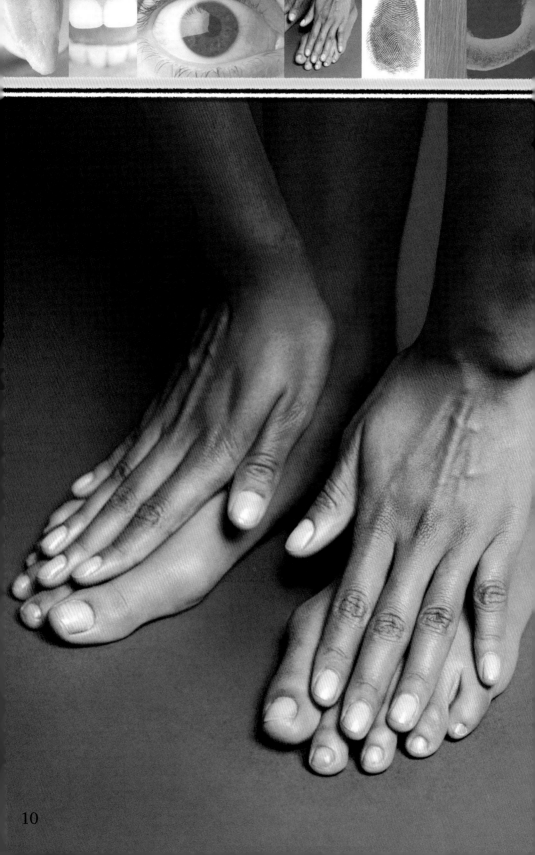

Fingernails and Toenails

Fingernails and toenails
are made from cells of hard skin.
They guard the ends of your
fingers and toes.
Nails grow from the base to the tip.
Each nail has a light half-moon shape
at its base.
Your nail starts to grow from this area.

Weird Facts

- Fingernails grow faster than toenails.
- It takes about six months for nails to grow from base to tip.

Fingerprint and Iris

Parts of your body are different
from everyone else's.
You have lines on the tips of your fingers.
These lines are called *fingerprints*.
No one else has your fingerprint.

The circle of color in your eye
is called the *iris*.
It controls light coming into the eye.
No one else has
an iris like yours.

Weird Facts

- If you hurt your fingertip, the skin will grow back with the same fingerprint!
- People with no color in their eyes are called *albinos*. Their irises are pinkish-gray.

13

Hair

Your hair is a lot like animals' fur.
It keeps your body warm.
Hair grows from tiny holes in your skin.
These holes are called *follicles*.
Straight hair grows out
of round follicles.
Curly hair grows out of flat follicles.
There are three million hairs
on the human body.

Weird Facts

- Beards have the fastest-growing hair. A beard could grow to be 30 feet long over a lifetime.

- People have hair on most parts of their bodies. They do not have hair on the palms of their hands, bottoms of feet, or lips.

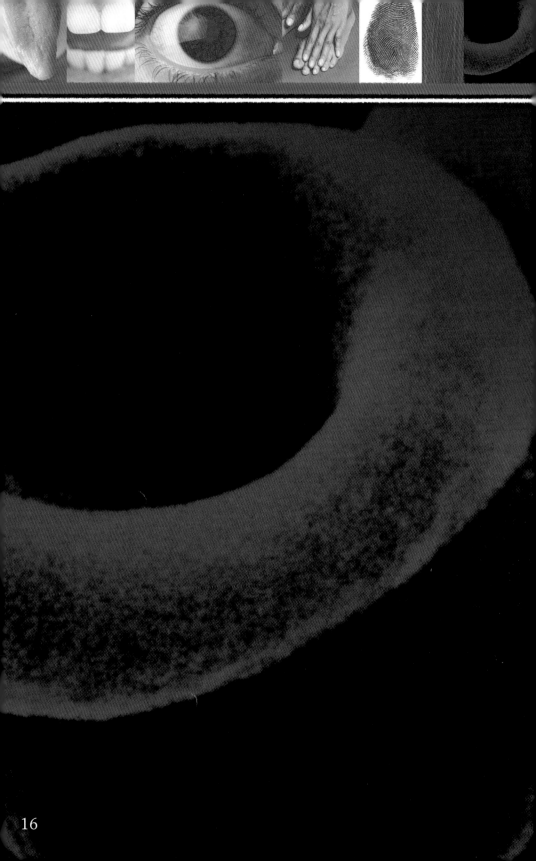

Blood

Blood works hard to keep you healthy.
It flows through the body in tubes.
They are called *vessels*.
Blood carries food throughout
your body.
It carries oxygen to your cells.
It carries away waste that the body
does not need.

Weird Facts

- All people do not have the same kind of blood.
  Blood is sorted into four types— *A, B, AB,* and *O.*
  The most common blood type in the world is *O.*

- The average person has 30 billion
  red blood cells.

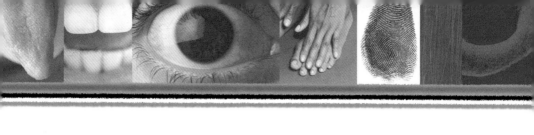

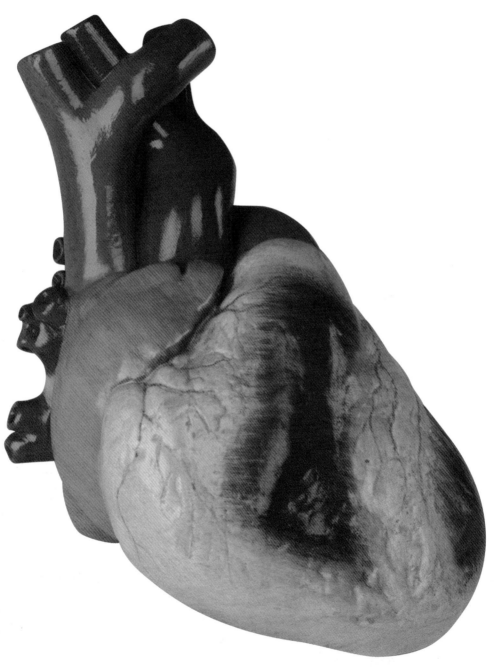

Heart

Your heart is made of special muscle.
It sends blood throughout the body.
The heart has two pumps.
One sends blood to your body.
One sends blood to your lungs.
It makes a pumping sound
called a *heartbeat*.

Weird Facts

- A baby's heart beats faster than an adult's. A baby's heart beats 135 times a minute. An adult's heart beats about 70 times a minute.

- There are more heart attacks on Mondays than on any other day of the week.

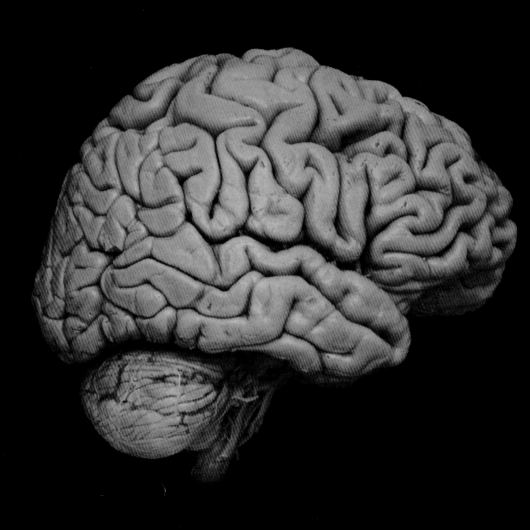

Brain

The brain is the control center
of your body.
It directs the way you think and act.
Your brain has two halves.
The right half controls
the left side of the body.
The left half controls
the right side of the body.
The brain is a grayish-pink color.
It weighs about three pounds.

Weird Facts

- The brain is made of nerve cells. Yet, it has no sensory nerves of its own. Your brain cannot feel pleasure or pain.

- The brain is wrinkled. This allows it to fit inside the skull.

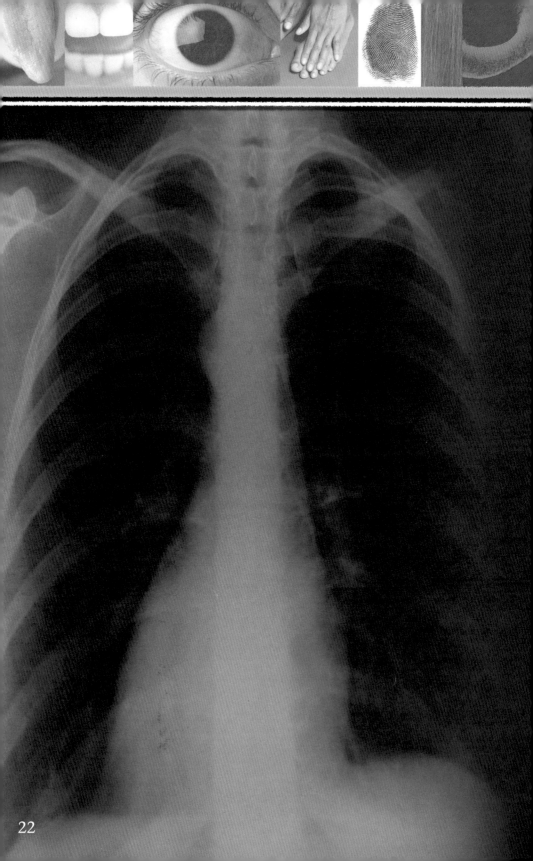

Lungs

Your lungs help you breathe.
They keep you alive.
The body cannot hold onto air
for a long time.
It always needs a new supply.
When you breathe in,
your lungs get bigger.
Air flows into your body.
Fresh air gives you power
to work and play.

Weird Facts

- No matter how hard you breathe out, you cannot force all the air out of your lungs.

- There are seven million alveoli, or tiny air sacs, in your lungs. If spread out flat, they could cover a tennis court.

Muscles

Your body has over 600 muscles.
These muscles work together.
They stretch and bend
to help you move.
When muscles are used,
they grow bigger.
Muscles also need rest,
just like you.

Weird Facts

- You use muscles in your sleep. People change position about 35 times a night.

- Without muscles, your face would have no expression.

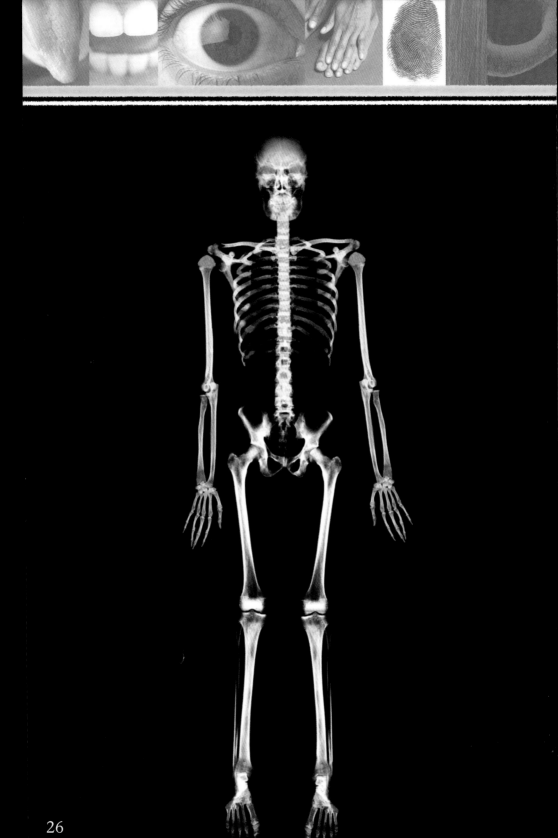

Skeleton

Walls give a house its shape.
The skeleton gives your body
its shape.
There are 206 bones in the skeleton.
They guard your heart, brain,
and lungs.
When two bones come together,
they form a joint.
Joints let you bend, walk, and run.

Weird Facts

- Almost 25 percent of your bones are in your feet!

- Babies are born with 300 bones. Adults have 206 bones. As you grow, some bones join together.

27

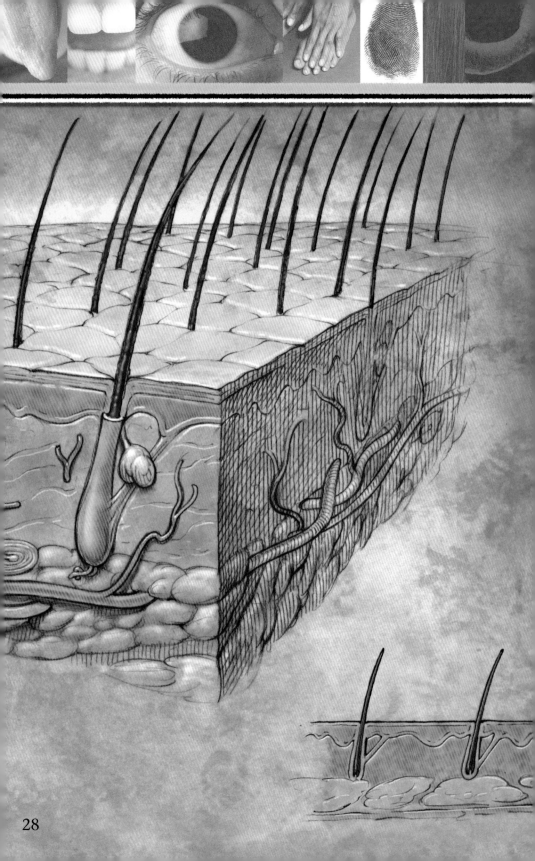

Skin

Your skin is the largest organ
in your body.
It helps you stay healthy.
Your skin keeps out dirt and germs.
It keeps in body fluids.
It also keeps your body from getting
too warm or too cold.
New skin grows all the time.

Weird Facts

- Every hour, a person loses about 600,000 skin cells.
- There are 45 miles of nerves in your skin.

Excuse Me!

Sometimes, your body is surprising.
A hiccup is a sudden intake of air.
The longest case of hiccups on record
lasted 69 years!
A sneeze is a sudden rush of air out of
the nose and mouth.
It can travel over 100 miles per hour.
When you have too much gas in
your stomach, it must come out.
Most people release a pint of intestinal
gas a day!

Weird Facts

- In a lifetime, a person produces enough spit to fill two swimming pools.
- A snore can be almost as loud as a power drill.

EXTREME FACTS ABOUT THE BIZARRE BODY!

- Your tongue has about 9,000 taste buds. You lose taste buds as you grow older!

- Once in every 2,000 births, a baby is born with a tooth.

- The average person blinks nearly five million times a year.

- If you are right-handed, the nails on your right hand grow faster than the nails on your left hand.

- In some parts of the world, iris identification is used instead of drivers' licenses or passports.

- Hair is as strong as aluminum. A rope of hair could lift a car.

- Your body has over 60,000 miles of blood vessels. This is enough to circle the earth two times.

- Your heart beats 100,000 times a day.

- The human brain is approximately 85 percent water.

- Adult lungs can hold nine pints of air.

- The muscles in human fingers flex 25 million times over the course of a lifetime.

- Thighbones are stronger than concrete.

- Most house dust is made of dead skin cells.

- A cough can move air over 1,000 feet per second, close to the speed of sound.